QUILTING IS MY THERAPY

Behind the Stitches with Angela Walters

stash BOOKS®

an imprint of C&T Publishing

Text copyright © 2016 by Angela Walters

Photography and artwork copyright © 2016 by C&T Publishing, Inc.

PUBLISHER: Amy Marson

CREATIVE DIRECTOR: Gailen Runge

EDITOR: Liz Aneloski

COVER/BOOK DESIGNER: April Mostek

PRODUCTION COORDINATORS:
Tim Manibusan and Zinnia Heinzmann

PRODUCTION EDITORS:
Jennifer Warren and Nicole Rolandelli

PHOTO ASSISTANT: Carly Jean Marin

PHOTOGRAPHY by Diane Pedersen of
C&T Publishing, unless otherwise noted

Published by Stash Books, an imprint of C&T Publishing, Inc.,
P.O. Box 1456, Lafayette, CA 94549

Library of Congress Cataloging-in-Publication Data
Names: Walters, Angela, 1979- author.
Title: Quilting is my therapy--behind the stitches with Angela Walters / Angela Walters.
Description: Lafayette, CA : C&T Publishing, Inc., [2016]
Identifiers: LCCN 2016023656 | ISBN 9781617455162 (soft cover)
Subjects: LCSH: Quilting. | Machine quilting. | Walters, Angela, 1979---Anecdotes.
Classification: LCC TT835 .W356557 2016 | DDC 746.46--dc23
LC record available at https://lccn.loc.gov/2016023656

Printed in China

10 9 8 7 6 5 4 3 2 1

DEDICATION

To Grandpa Ford—

without you, none of this would have been possible.

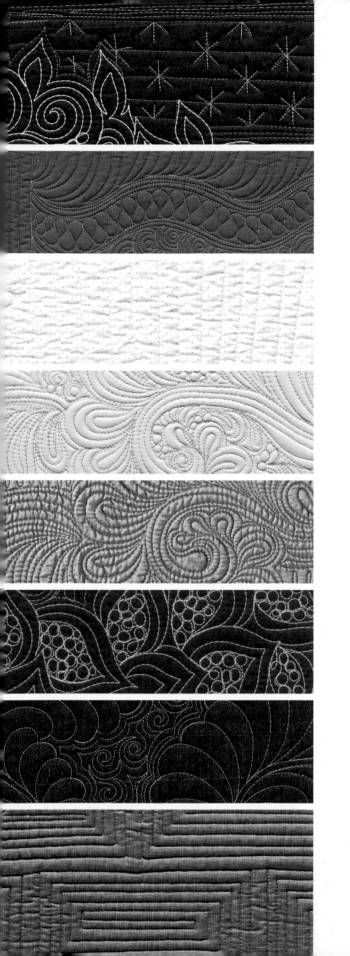

CONTENTS

INTRODUCTION

There is nothing quite like running your hand over a quilt. The feel of the quilting is like music to my soul. Quilting provides a specific function—holding the layers together—but it is so much more than that. It enhances the quilt top by adding another layer of art to the quilt. Quilting can bring out secondary patterns, tell a story, or add a pop of color. Most of the time, quilting plays off of the quilt top. But sometimes, like in this book, it can take center stage.

I have compiled some of my favorite quilts that show the range of my designs. As you look through the book, I hope that you will be inspired, not intimidated. You might notice that my quilting isn't perfect—that's because quilting isn't supposed to be. As

Quilting can bring out secondary patterns, tell a story, or add a pop of color.

you work on your quilt tops, don't strive for perfection; strive for completion, remembering that a finished quilt is always better than a perfectly quilted one.

Sprinkled among the photographs are little bits about my journey from fast-food manager (true story) to professional machine quilter. I hope you will enjoy it as much as I have enjoyed reliving my journey.

STARTING FROM THE BEGINNING

Have you ever heard of the phrase, "Even a blind squirrel gets a nut sometimes"? It pretty much sums up my quilting career. Like most professionals in the quilting industry, I didn't set out to be a professional quilter. It's not as though that option is in the list of potential careers.

I didn't grow up with family members that quilted, and I was never crafty—well, at least in the sense of making things. In fact, I failed the sewing machine test in eighth grade home economics ... twice. All I had to do was identify the parts of sewing machine; I didn't have to actually use it! If I am being honest, the only reason I passed the third time was because the teacher finally took pity on me and helped "suggest" some of the answers. So when I say, "If I can do it, anyone can," you can take me at my word.

I didn't actually know what a quilt was until I met my husband, Jeremy.

I didn't actually know what a quilt was until I met my husband, Jeremy. His grandparents started quilting after retirement. It was quite amazing, actually. His grandpa made quilts as a way to entice family members to attend the annual family reunion. He pieced and hand quilted a quilt for every generation. To win one of the quilts, a family member had to attend the reunion and could only win a quilt once. I would soon learn why these rules were so important.

I wasn't even married to Jeremy when I attended my first family reunion. It was there that I got the first glimpse of how coveted these quilts were. If you have ever been to a family gathering where things got tense over, let's say, potato salad, you can imagine what happens when the stakes are as high as a quilt.

I won't say that it was violent or anything, but there was a lot of passive-aggressive complaining. "Didn't Aunt Martha already win a quilt?" and "Why does her family always win?" were just a few of the comments made. I remember looking around and thinking, "Geez, people! These are just blankets!" I know now that saying such a thing is sacrilegious in quilting. I just want to show how ignorant I was at the time.

Jeremy didn't win a quilt at the reunion, so on a whim I asked Grandpa to show me how to make one. He assured me that even though I had *no* sewing experience, I could learn how to do it. One thing I want to point out is that he said, "Yes." He didn't say, "Yes, but you need to make the quilt I want you to make using the fabric I like." He didn't judge my choice of fabric or pattern, which is something I think all quilters should do when sharing their love of quilting.

He said, "Yes." He didn't say, "Yes, but you need to make the quilt I want you to make using the fabric I like."

Grandpa started me off on a nine-patch quilt, and I remember making that first Nine-Patch block vividly. He had a 4″ square template and taught me how to trace the shape onto the fabric, cut it out, and piece my first-ever quilt block. About an hour later, I held up my nine-patch (which wasn't horrible, if I do say so myself). With his eyes gleaming, he exclaimed, "Wonderful job! Now let me show you the easy way." Then he pulled out his rotary cutter and ruler. Thank goodness that he did, because I don't think I would be a quilter today if I had to use templates! That first nine-patch quilt is still on my bed.

So it began: I was addicted to quilting. We hand quilted the first several quilts I made. Grandpa gave me a frame, and he, Jeremy, and I sat side by side and quilted. He would tell us stories and we would have a great time. I wish I had taken pictures during this time, but I was too busy enjoying the moment.

BAUBLE

designed by Emily Cier

The name sums up this quilt perfectly—it's bright and fun, just like a well-loved bauble. Quilting this was just like a "choose your own adventure." There were so many different ways to go about combining the blocks.

QUILTING IS MY THERAPY

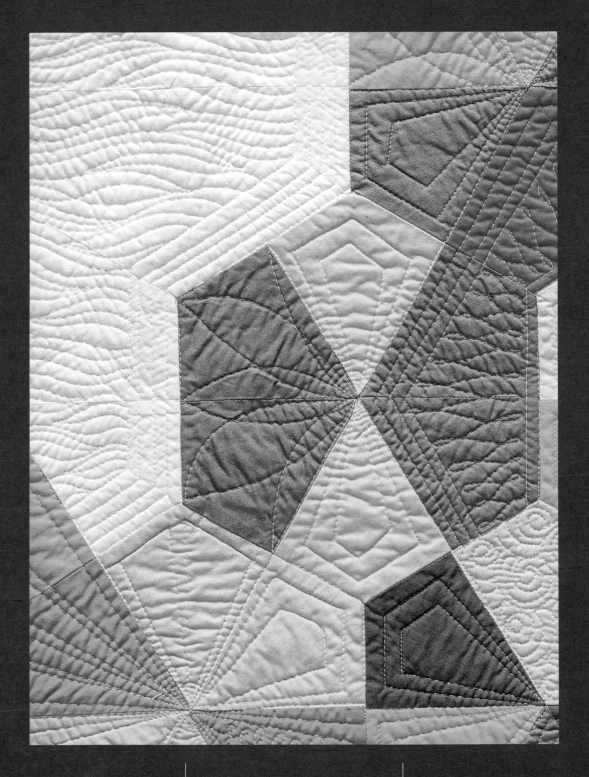

BAUBLE designed by Emily Cier.

BUTTERFLY
designed by Tula Pink

This was such a daunting quilt top to machine quilt. Not only was it intricate and gorgeously pieced, but it also contained so much negative space to work with. It was Tula's idea to quilt the feathers to look like antennae—so of course I ran with the concept.

BUTTERFLY
designed by Tula Pink

What's better than a beautifully quilted feather? A super-sized feather! Exaggerating the size helped to make a bold statement and filled in the area quickly. Echo quilting and the dense filler completed the look.

With so much dramatic quilting in the negative space, I kept the quilting in the blocks more basic. But just because the quilting is basic doesn't mean it isn't impactful.

FROM HAND QUILTER TO MACHINE QUILTER

I didn't hate hand quilting, but I didn't love it either. Jeremy and Grandpa were way better at it than I was; I was content to just hang out and pretend to quilt. But one day about two years later, everything changed. While hanging out at his house, Grandpa said, "I think you should get a longarm quilting machine." I quickly answered, "I think I should too … what is it?" It turns out he didn't know what one was either, having only seen one from afar at a quilt show. Despite our complete lack of knowledge of quilting machines, Grandpa was undeterred. He ordered some information from a company, and we began looking over the options.

"I think you should get a longarm quilting machine." I quickly answered, "I think I should too … what is it?"

When I found out that the company had a used machine available, I was giddy and ready to make it mine. Jeremy, understandably, was more hesitant. Thankfully, Grandpa interceded and pulled rank, telling him, "If you don't buy her one, I'll buy it for her." What could Jeremy do? Everyone wanted to make Grandpa happy, so if Grandpa said buy a longarm, you bought a longarm.

I'd like to take a moment and point out that this isn't how I would suggest buying any kind of machine, especially one as big as a longarm! But like I said, I was just a blind squirrel. Thankfully it worked out.

To say that we were excited about the longarm would be an understatement. While we waited for my baby to arrive, we tried to figure out how it worked. That's right—not only had I *never* seen one but I had never even machine quilted. Finally we decided that it must be computerized. Really, how else could it work? It made stars and loopy designs; it was really the only way. I'll wait here while you chuckle at my ignorance. ...

I quickly realized that not only was it not computerized but I also had to hand-guide the thing.

I am sure you can imagine the look on my face when the machine was delivered. I quickly realized that not only was it not computerized but I also had to hand-guide the thing. There I was, surrounded by Grandpa, Jeremy, and a few other family members. I had to act as though I wasn't scared out of my mind. The gentleman that set up the machine showed me how to load the machine, how to thread it, and how to quilt a meander. Then ... he was gone.

You may wonder why I didn't just machine quilt on my sewing machine. That answer is simple: we didn't know it was possible. Every day I thank God that we didn't know we could, because there is no way I could have talked Jeremy into buying a longarm otherwise.

Luckily for me, Grandpa suffered from a particular eye condition— he never saw an ugly quilt top.

Luckily for me, Grandpa suffered from a particular eye condition—he never saw an ugly quilt top. If it had at least two pieces of fabric sewed together, he was going to buy it. Whether at a flea market, a thrift store, or an auction, if he saw a "quilt top," he was going to get it. It didn't matter who got in front of his motorized scooter. He was going to run them over in pursuit of the treasure. By the time I received my quilting machine, he had amassed a stack of at least 30 quilt tops. They were real "beauties": hand-pieced, double-knit grandmother's flower garden quilt tops. (Just in case you can't tell, I am being sarcastic.)

Once the machine was set up and the technician left, I took off the practice quilt sandwich and loaded my first quilt top. Even though it had been only a few hours since the techician had left, I wasn't scared. I figured I couldn't make these quilt tops look any worse! I didn't realize it then, but I was beginning the next phase of my quilting "career."

I could lie to you and say that machine quilting came effortless to me. I could imply that the machine glided as though it were an extension of my body. But that wouldn't be true. Since I was self-taught, I had an idiot for a teacher. I made so many mistakes! For one, I loaded a quilt back that was too short for the quilt top. Not realizing this until I got to the end of the quilt, I did the only rational thing. I cut the last border off of the quilt. I can see myself giving the quilt to Grandpa afterward and saying, "Sorry it's not quite right; the backing was just too small." Grandpa, the sweetest and most encouraging person I knew, simply replied, "It's perfect!"

So it continued. I quilted Grandpa's quilt tops, butchering most of them. No matter what, he would always tell me that they were the best quilts ever. That was the key element to my success. I didn't have YouTube or free tutorials; Grandpa was the only quilter I knew. He said I was the best ever, and I believed it. I am so thankful that I didn't have anything to compare myself to. I didn't have to drool over pictures of other people's quilting. I wasn't bombarded with Instagram pictures of gorgeous designs. I was blissfully ignorant that anyone else in the world was quilting, and I just enjoyed the process of learning how to machine quilt.

I quilted the whole stack of quilts and presented Grandpa with the bill of $130. It may not seem like enough for 30-plus quilts, but since I ruined most of them and it was because of him that I had the machine, I decided it was fair enough.

I was blissfully ignorant that anyone else in the world was quilting, and I just enjoyed the process of learning how to machine quilt.

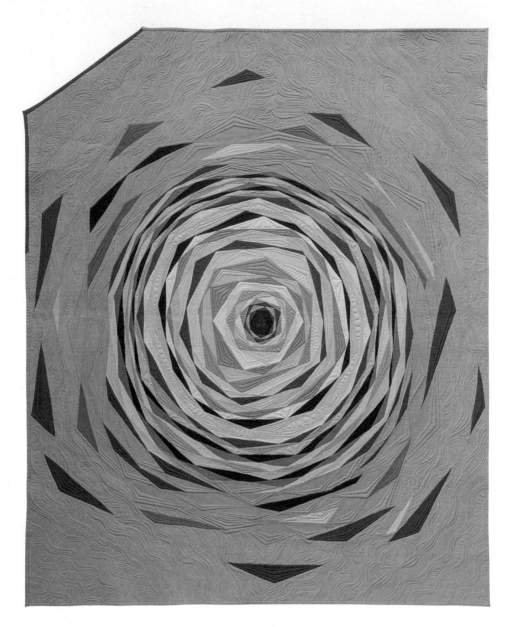

IMPRACTICALITY
by Angela Walters

I named this quilt *Impracticality* because making it was an impractical use of
time and fabric, but I enjoyed every minute. Quilting it was a little harder than
piecing it—I wasn't sure what to do with all the negative space. I ended up using
the quilting designs to "complete" the quilt pattern and then used contrasting
wavy lines to surround the center.

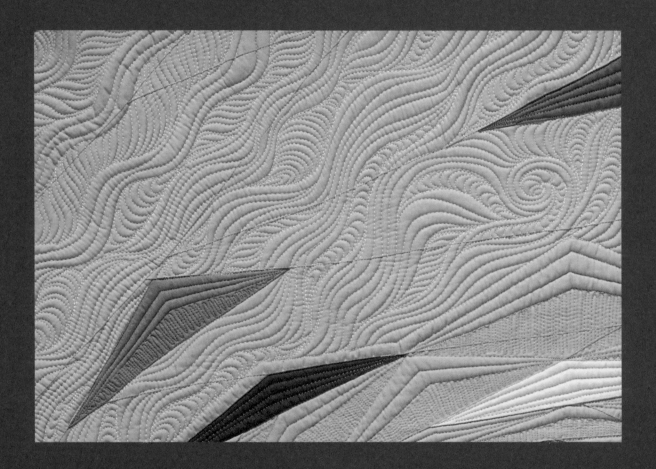

IMPRACTICALITY by Angela Walters

I am sometimes asked if it is possible to have too many quilting designs on a quilt. I'm sure it is, but I have just never seen it happen. To keep designs from overwhelming a quilt top, it helps to use a thread color that matches the quilt.

I just love how the quilted triangles stand out from each other. Using contrasting designs prevents them from blending into each other.

DRAWN
by Angela Walters

No matter how long one has been quilting, there are always new things to learn. *Drawn* provided an opportunity to try a new-to-me technique of using two threads at the same time. I enjoyed playing with combining colors and textures. This quilt is a great reminder to always keep experimenting.

Using two layers of
wool batting really
made the feather
designs pop out!

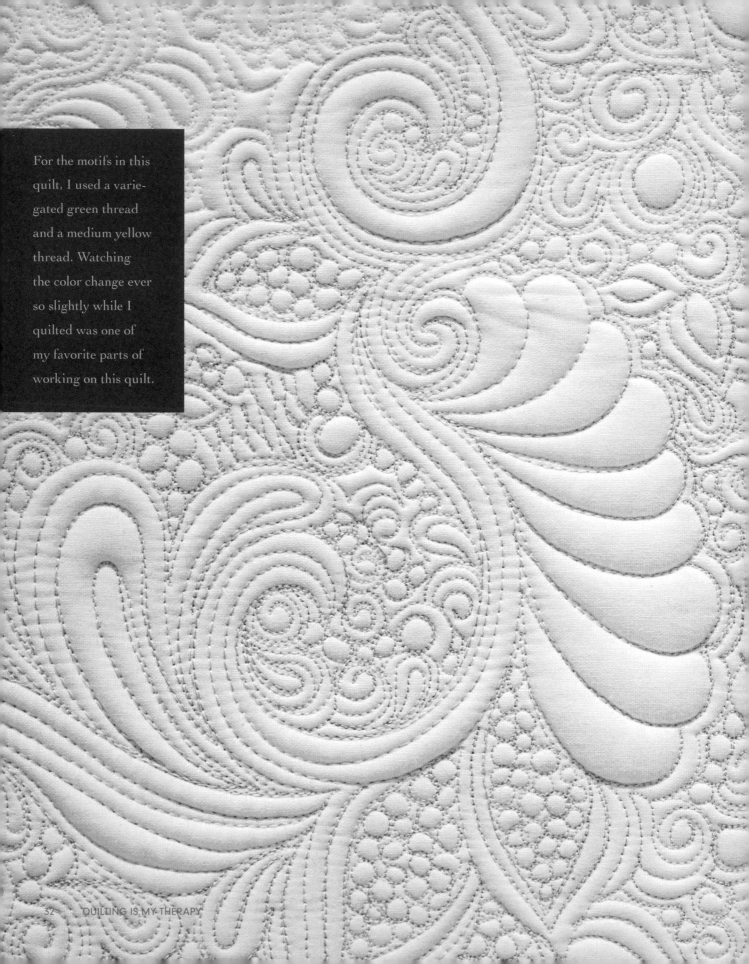

For the motifs in this quilt, I used a variegated green thread and a medium yellow thread. Watching the color change ever so slightly while I quilted was one of my favorite parts of working on this quilt.

DRAWN by Angela Walters

It's amazing to me how using slightly different shades of thread adds depth to one's quilting. I used four different shades of red thread in the letters. It just goes to show that if quilting is my therapy, then threads are my medication!

GOING PRO

After I finished Grandpa's quilts and the few quilt tops that I had hanging around, I realized I had nothing else to machine quilt. So I had two options: I could piece more quilt tops, or I could become a "professional" quilter and quilt other people's. Now, if the last section could be called "How Not to Buy a Quilting Machine," this section would be "How Not to Go into Business." Same blind squirrel, another nut.

Joining a group seemed a bit scary, but since I didn't worry about looking silly, I jumped right in.

Not surprisingly, I decided to go into business for myself. In my opinion, the less piecing I had to do the better. After convincing Jeremy that I was indeed serious, I hopped on the computer and went to Ask.com to figure out how to start a machine-quilting business. (That was before Google; that's how long it's been.) One website suggested joining a local quilt guild. Hmm … brilliant! Up to that point, I didn't know any other quilters besides Grandpa. Joining a group seemed a bit scary, but since I didn't worry about looking silly, I jumped right in.

I attended my first local quilt guild meeting after deciding to go into business. I even had some very lame business cards made up just in case. That very first meeting had two significant results. I realized that, at 24, I was a lot younger than the average quilter and that quilt guilds held their own quilt shows. So I did what anyone else would do—I volunteered to be a vendor at the show. I did this despite never having gone to a quilt show … ever … in my life. What was the worst that could happen?

I'll tell you the worst thing that could happen. You could show up as a vendor. You could bring your quilt (one quilt!) and business cards. You could set them up on the table and have a seat, then slowly start to realize that other vendors are driving trailer loads up to the back loading dock. You could feel a chill as you realize how unprepared and pathetic you might look sitting there, by yourself, in your empty booth. But knowing it's too late, all you can do is smile and hope for the best. Which is exactly what happened. I sat there all weekend, met a few great people, and gave out a few business cards, which were taken most likely out of pity. I did get one customer from the show. I'll tell you more about her later.

But knowing it's too late, all you can do is smile and hope for the best. Which is exactly what happened.

Ultimately the show was a bust. I could have given up right then, but I didn't. I wanted to see if I could get just one customer. So, I kept attending guild meetings and actually started getting a few customers (much to my surprise). I will never, ever forget getting paid for the first quilt. I held the $35 check up to my hubby and said, "We are going out to dinner!" Just writing about it now brings a smile to my face. I had met the one and only goal I had set for myself.

My business didn't take off like a rocket ship. It was more like a snowball rolling down a hill, starting small and gradually getting bigger. After a couple of years, I had enough business to keep me busy. I loved the fact that I got to work from home and make money doing what I loved. I truly was living the American dream.

REJECT
designed by Tula Pink

Named by Tula Pink, *Reject* can't help but make me smile. I wanted the quilting to enhance the block letters, so I opted for straight lines that followed the edges of the block. I love the 3-D look it adds to the quilt. And because we both love swirls and feathers, I definitely had to use them in the background.

In my opinion, great quilting enhances a quilt without taking away from it. That's why I usually use thread that matches the fabric. In the maroon parts of this quilt I used red thread, and in the rest of the quilt I used a neutral color. It took a little longer, but the result was well worth the effort.

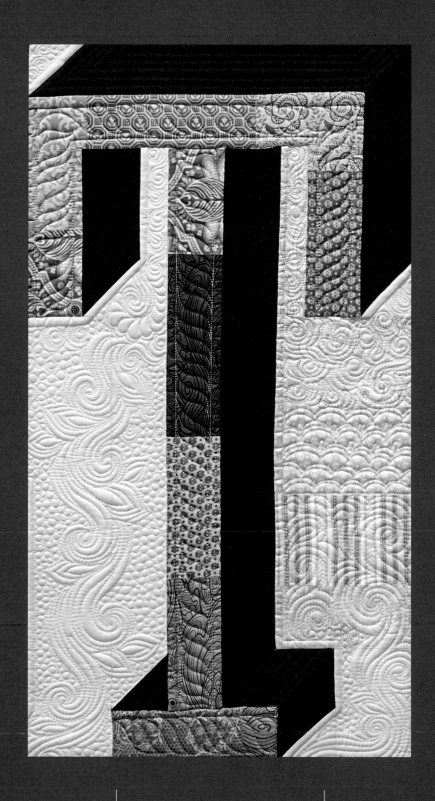

REJECT designed by Tula Pink

RADIANCE
by Angela Walters

One secret to great quilting is to use a shiny fabric. Even if the quilting isn't perfect, people will be so distracted by the fabric that they won't see any mistakes. This quilt is actually a sampler showing all the variations of the paisley feather, one of my favorite quilting designs.

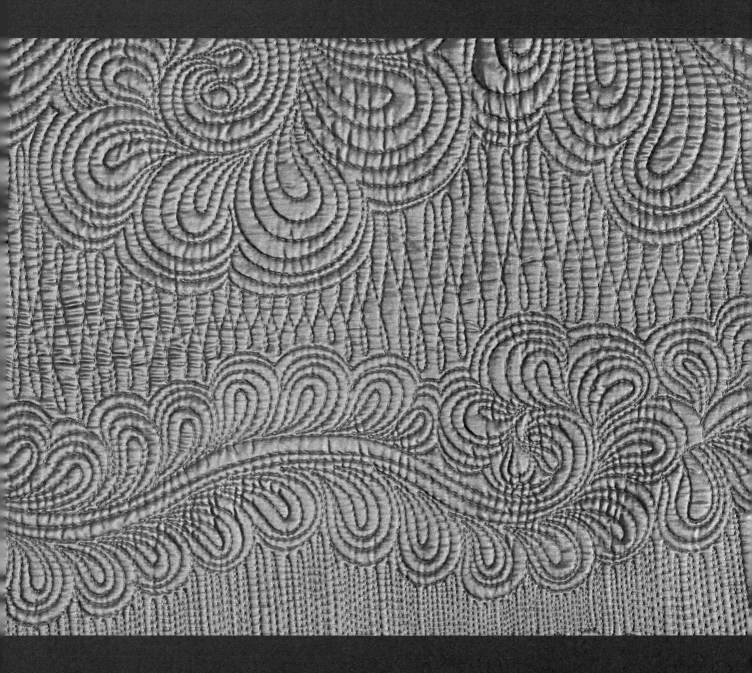

Wishbones aren't just for borders and sashing. I also like to use them as fillers between other quilting designs. ·

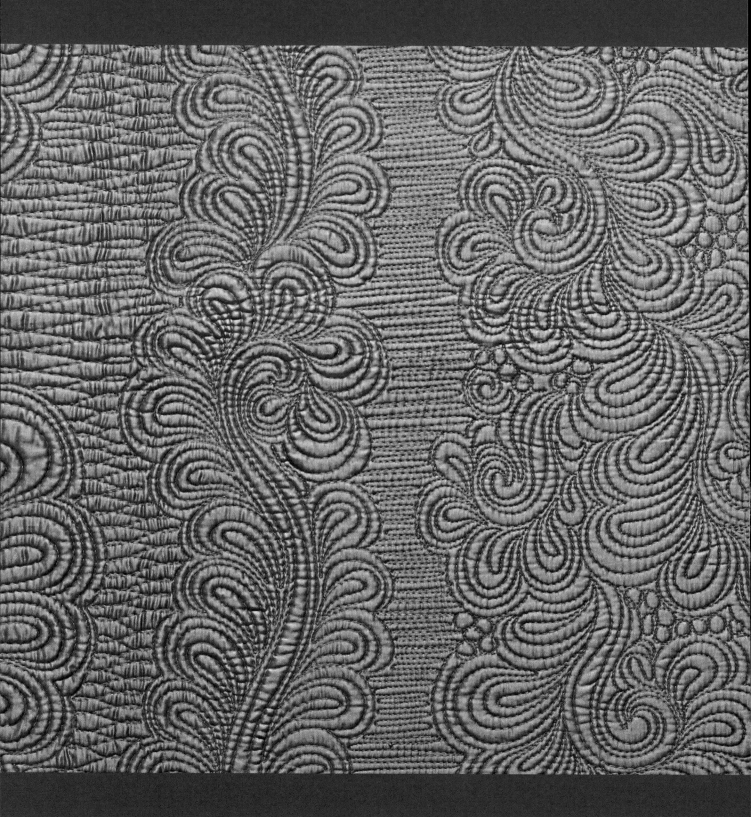

RADIANCE by Angela Walters

PEAKS AND VALLEYS

designed by Tula Pink

"I want it quilted unlike anything we have seen before" is what Tula Pink said when we discussed ways to quilt her gorgeous *Peaks and Valleys*. No pressure, right? While we both love a great feather, I opted for some angular geometric quilting designs. The best part? I was able to quilt the whole quilt without marking any designs. That's a win/win in my book!

GOING PRO   45

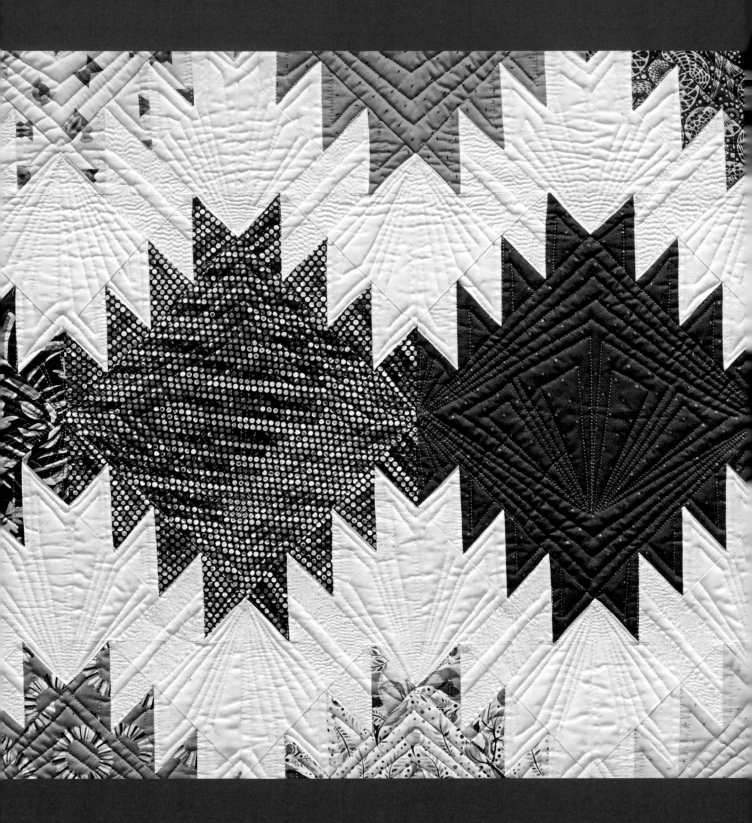

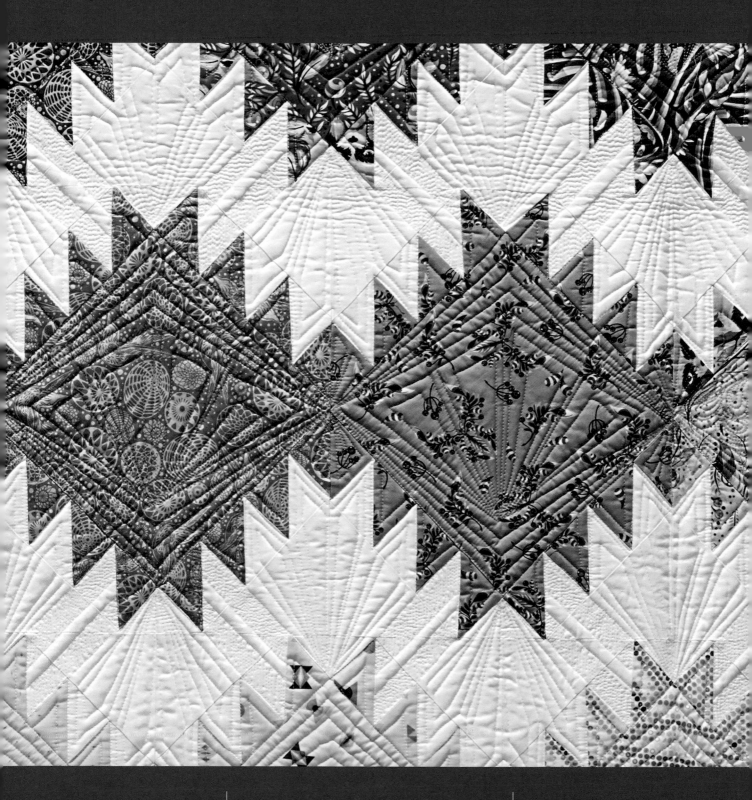

PEAKS AND VALLEYS designed by Tula Pink

INSPIRE
by Angela Walters

I love looking at graffiti, whether on buildings, signs, or even trains. Inspired, I decided to make a quilt that looked like graffiti. The actual quilt top is minimally pieced, leaving space for the fun part—the quilting. After quilting the word in the center and the rest of the filler designs, I painted the letters. The painting process took longer than the quilting, which led me to declare that I would never paint another quilt again. You'll soon see that I didn't stick to that declaration (see *Legacy*, page 66).

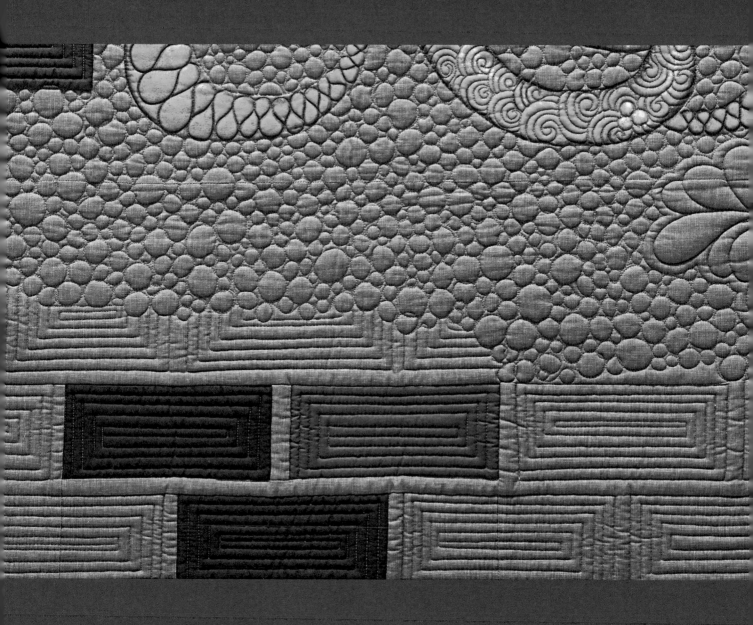

I am easily amused and get a lot of joy from quilting designs in different ways. I love how the pebble quilting looks as though it's going over the top of the quilted "bricks." It really serves no purpose other than to make me smile!

INSPIRE by Angela Walters

The white paint adds a little highlight to the letters, giving them a rounded look. For the shadow, I used a permanent marker. What can I say? I didn't have any black paint!

GO BIG OR GO HOME

I would have happily continued quilting for my local customers until the end of time. But six years after I first started machine quilting, two things happened that changed the course of my career and my life: meeting Tula Pink and discovering the Modern Quilt Movement.

So remember— even if some- thing seems like a failure, you never know how it will turn out.

Remember how I said I got one customer from vending at the quilt show? That one customer was Kathy, and she picked up my card and called me a few months later. She was opening a new quilt shop and was wondering if I would like to quilt the samples. Um … of course! She quickly became a favorite customer of mine. A few years after opening her shop, she excitedly told me that her daughter was becoming a fabric designer. Kathy introduced us, and I began quilting for her daughter, otherwise known as Tula Pink. Just writing that now gives me chills. That first quilt show, which I did all those years ago, led to me quilting for Tula. So remember—even if something seems like a failure, you never know how it will turn out.

Tula and I like to joke that we are "married" to each other through quilting. The quilts we create together have resulted in my best work. In fact, you might notice that several of the quilts in this book are hers. It was my quilting in her booth that attracted the attention of C&T Publishing and ultimately led to me becoming an author.

Around the same time, I was invited to the first meeting of the Kansas City Modern Quilt Guild. It was there that I found out that there was such a thing as modern quilts, quilt blogs, and younger quilters in general. I was hooked!

If luck is just preparation meeting opportunity, then I sure was lucky. I was at the perfect place at the perfect time. Having been a machine quilter for several years, I had technical skill and an appreciation for traditional quilts. But I also loved the aesthetic of modern quilts. Looking at them, I could imagine so many ways to apply the quilting designs that I already knew.

It wasn't overnight, but I soon realized that I was in a position to take my business to the next level. I started reading books about business and goal setting. I began to get intentional about growing my business and pursuing as many opportunities as possible. Now that this blind squirrel had found her nut, she was going to go as far as she could.

I began to get intentional about growing my business and pursuing as many opportunities as possible.

COLOR FUSION

designed by Natalie Barnes

It's not often that I quilt a quilt with twelve sides. Instead of focusing on the individual pieces, I chose to use designs that wrapped around the whole quilt. Straight lines and ribbon candy are obviously some of my favorite go-to designs.

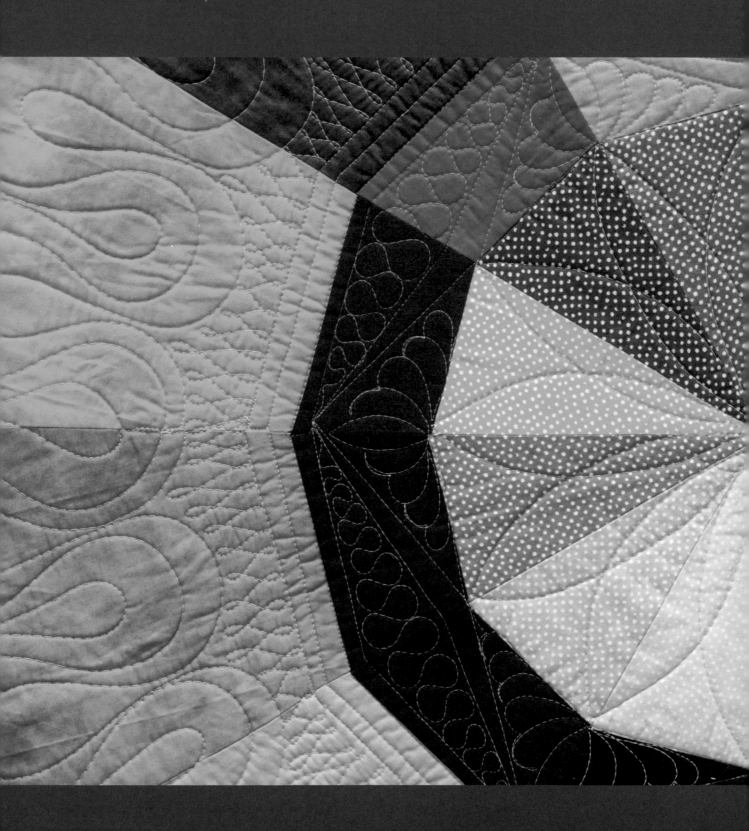

COLOR FUSION designed by Natalie Barnes

VENTANA
designed by Alison Glass

A quilt with repeating blocks and a lot of negative space is a dream come true to me!
Envisioning the secondary designs I could create with the quilting was almost as
fun as the quilting itself. I wasn't sure how *Ventana* would turn out when I started,
but sometimes not knowing what the end result will look like is half the fun.

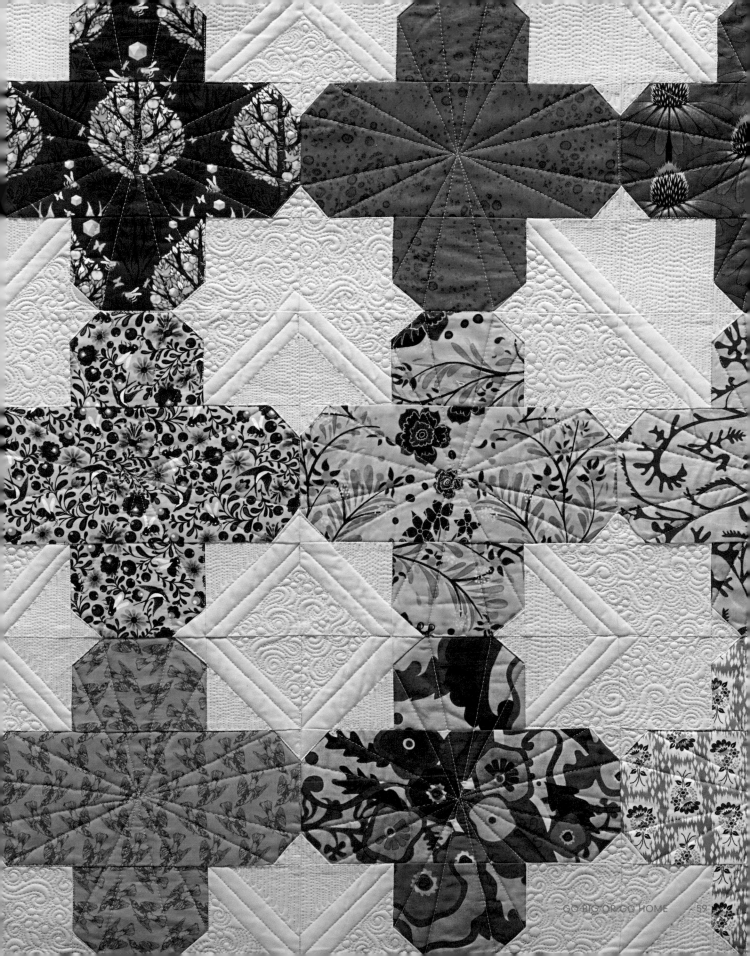

VENTANA designed by Alison Glass

Since the quilting in the negative space was so intricate and dense, I decided to keep the quilting in the blocks more basic. This helped to keep the quilting from hiding the beautiful print fabrics used in the quilt.

MINI-WHOLECLOTH
by Angela Walters

This quilt could also be called *The Deconstructed Dress*. I quilted this with the intent to turn it into a dress for a booth at a quilt convention. But when it came time to cut it, my mother-in-law (a master seamstress) said she couldn't do it. She ended up using pins to hold it together, which turned out great for me. I now have a wholecloth quilt.

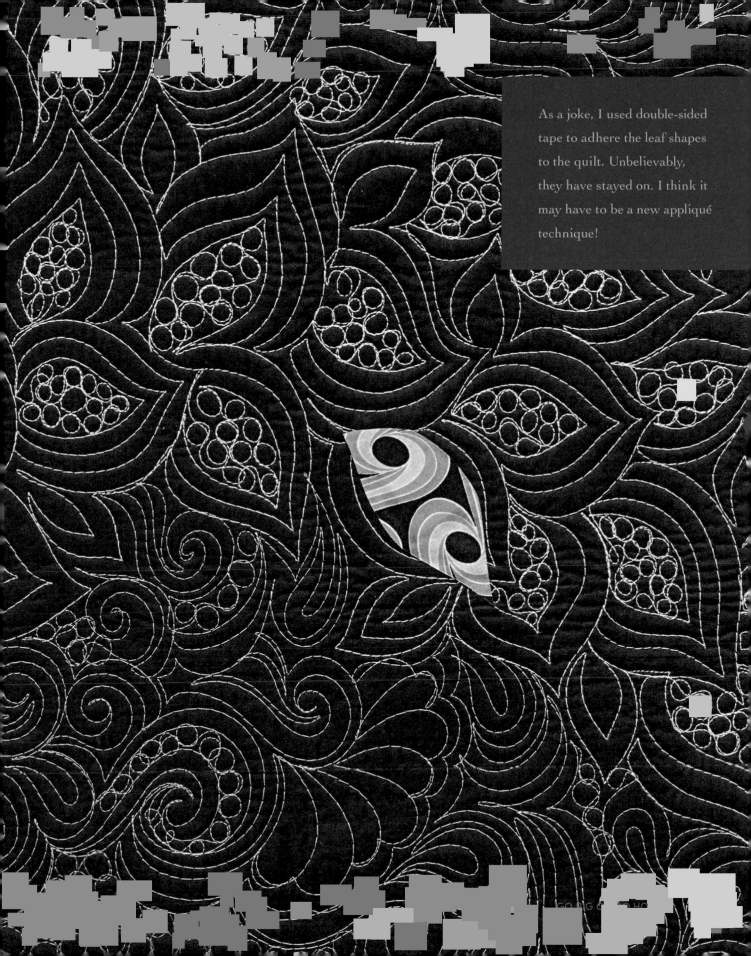

As a joke, I used double-sided tape to adhere the leaf shapes to the quilt. Unbelievably, they have stayed on. I think it may have to be a new appliqué technique!

MINI-WHOLECLOTH by Angela Walters

BACK TO THE FUTURE

One day in my studio, my middle child Cloe said wondrously, "You must have quilted a hundred quilts!" Laughing, I agreed that I had quilted at least a hundred quilts. I truly have no idea how many I have quilted, but I hope to have the opportunity to quilt twice as many.

I'm not sharing my story to tell you how great I am; I'm trying to show you how great you can be. If I can do it, anyone can. Now it's your turn! What "nut" are you looking for? Go out and get it!

Happy Quilting!

I am not sharing my story to tell you how great I am; I am trying to show you how great you can be.

LEGACY
by Angela Walters

While quilting *Inspire* (page 48), I vowed never to paint a quilt again. Needless to say, the vow didn't last long. I ended up using the same technique on *Legacy* to promote a fabric collection by the same name. Between the quilting and the painting, this quilt took forever! It's one of the biggest I have quilted. It ended up being too big to display in my house.

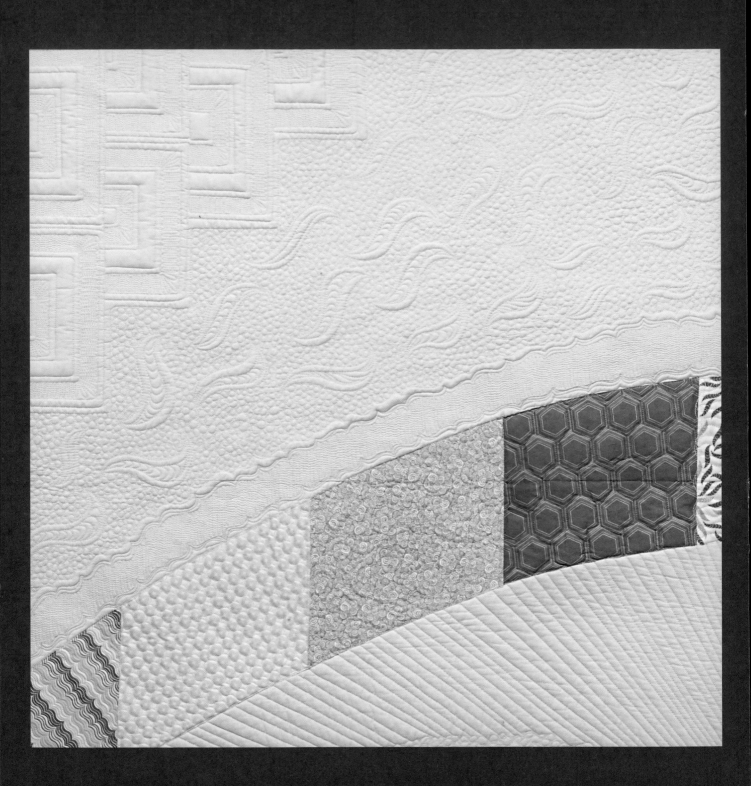

LEGACY by Angela Walters

Can you ever use too many quilting designs on a quilt? I guess so, but I have never actually seen it happen. I love to use several different designs on my quilts. They add interest to the quilt and keep me from getting too bored.

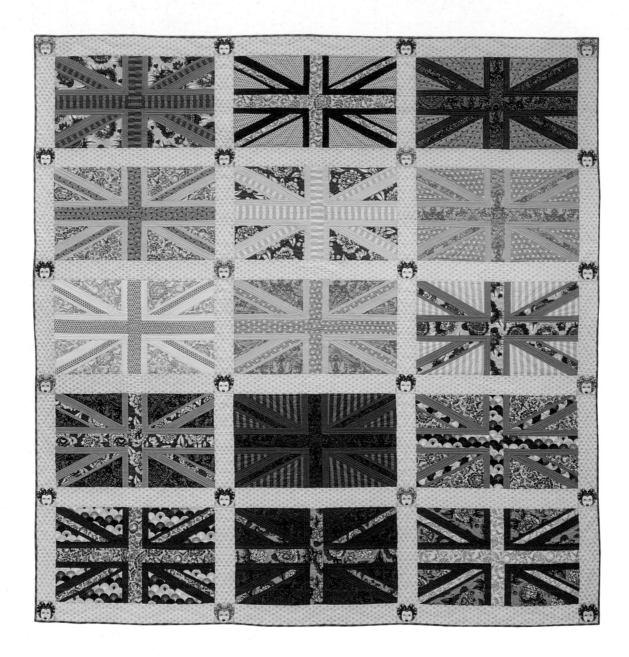

UNION JACK
designed by Tula Pink

Sometimes, the hardest thing about machine quilting is keeping myself reined in. I love over-the-top quilting with a lot of motifs and elements. But it's not always the best for the quilt. For *Union Jack*, I kept the quilting in the blocks fairly basic, while using more intricate designs in the sashing and borders to pull the blocks together and to create secondary designs.

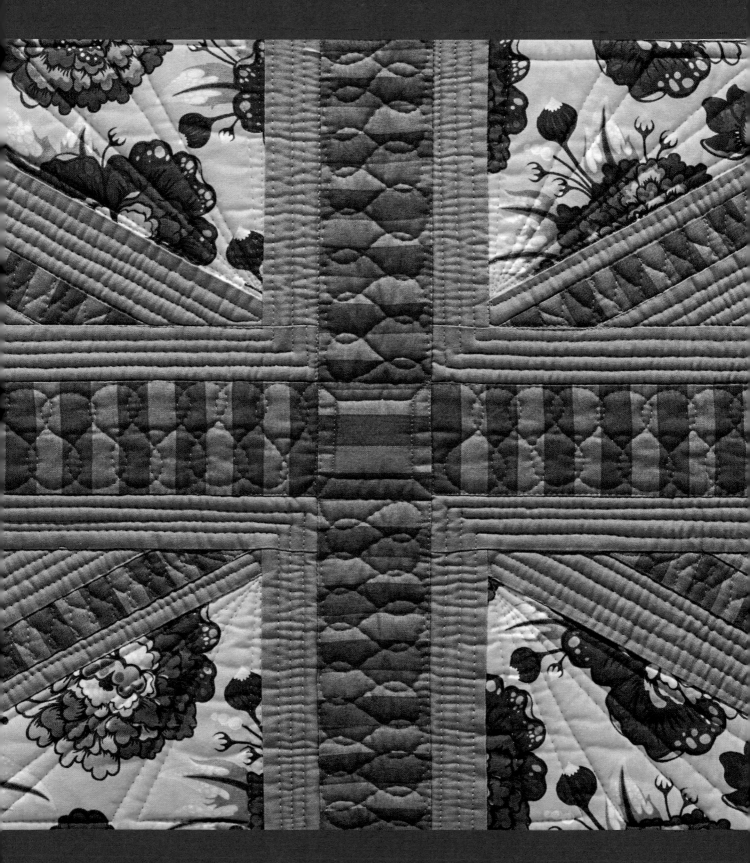

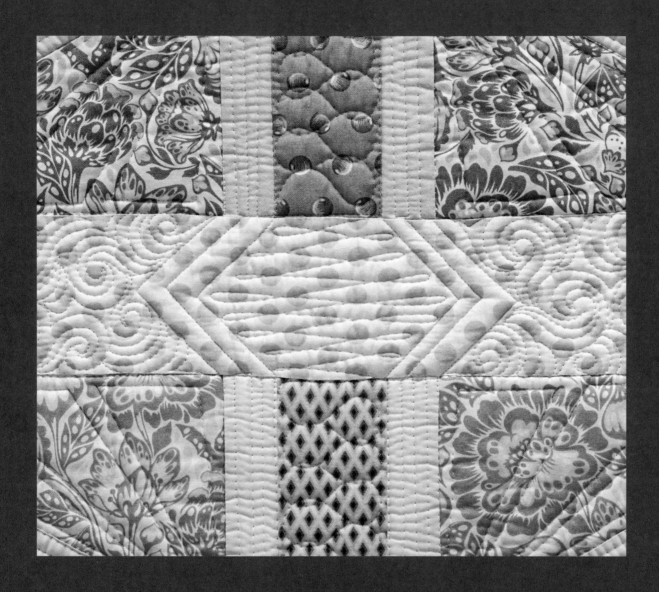

UNION JACK designed by Tula Pink

BACK TO THE FUTURE

UNION JACK
designed by Tula Pink

Don't underestimate the sashing on a quilt. The quilting between the blocks helps pull them together and also creates secondary designs. In this quilt, I combined diagonal lines and swirls to add interest to those areas. It was definitely more fun than just quilting one design!

I love quilting feathers that run off the edge of the quilt. There is something about it that just makes me smile.

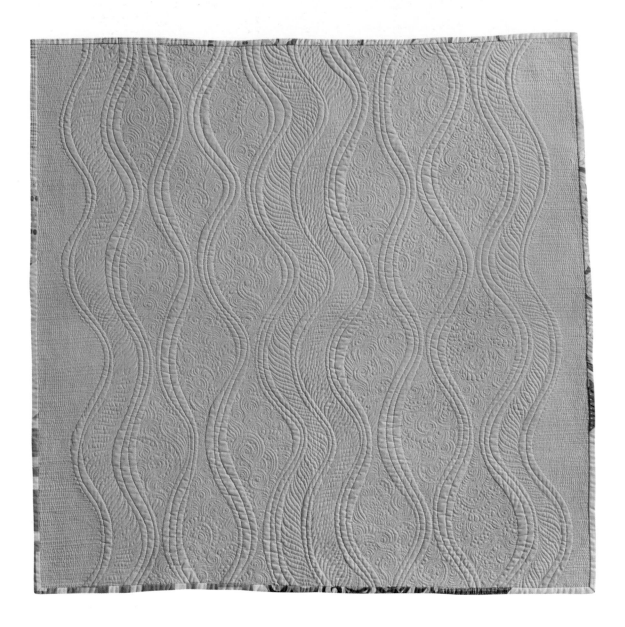

CREAM WHOLECLOTH
by Angela Walters

I often like to joke that the secret to great quilting is to quilt small and use matching thread (it doesn't matter how well you quilt if you can't see the designs!). While I am only half-joking, there is a kernel of truth to it. This wholecloth quilt is a great example of that. I used the wavy lines to break up the space and filled in between them with all my favorite quilting designs. This is a small quilt because I quickly became tired of quilting so tiny!

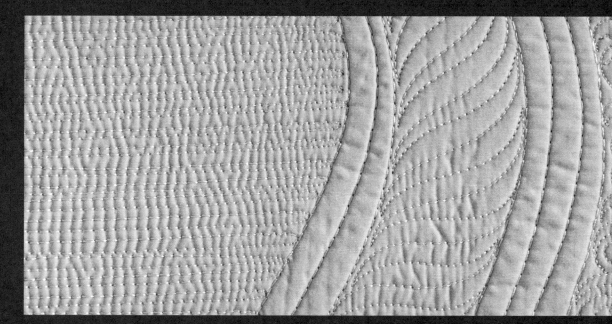

Matchstick quilting adds such a beautiful texture. It also changes things up a bit from the other areas of the quilt.

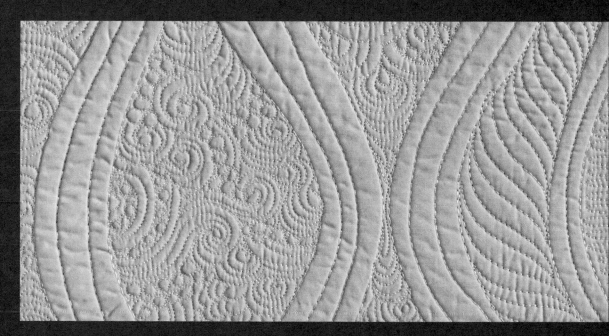

When I want the quilting to really "puff" out, I will use two layers of Quilter's Dream Poly batting. For this quilt, I tried a bamboo/silk blend instead. While it was luscious to quilt, I was disappointed when the designs didn't stand out. Now I know to stick with my poly batting if I happen to quilt

SPACE DUST
designed by Tula Pink

Quilt a giant ball turned spaceship? Why not? Working with fun quilts is the highlight of my career—whether it's adding fun details, such as a space alien, or playing off the angular shapes of the blocks. This quilt by Tula Pink still makes me smile!

A planet and a
shooting star add to
the theme of the quilt.

SPACE DUST
designed by Tula Pink

GOTHIC ARCHES
designed by Tula Pink

The inspiration behind a quilt top can play a huge role in which quilting designs I use. Knowing that the blocks in this quilt were meant to look like gothic arches made picking out the quilting designs easier!

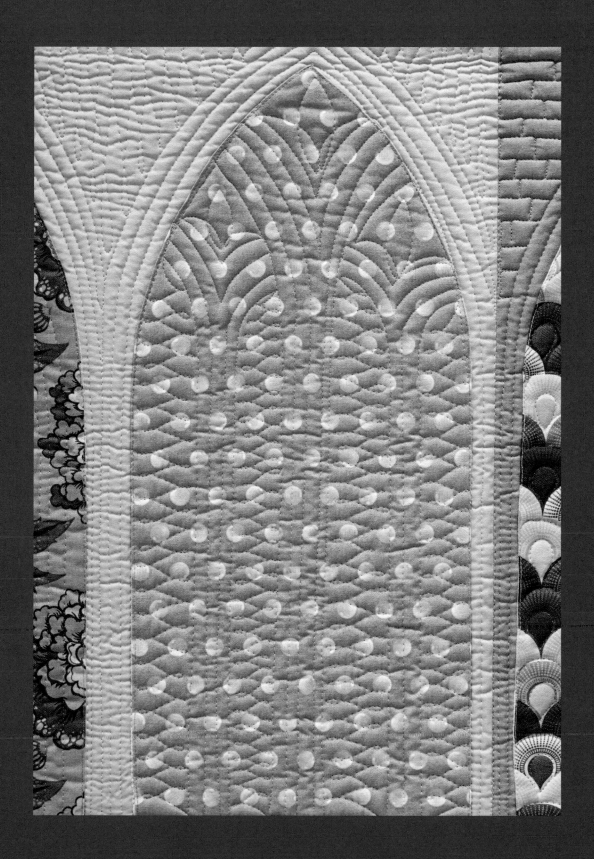

GOTHIC ARCHES designed by Tula Pink

Quilting little details, such as the bricks around the "gothic arch," makes me so happy. Keeping myself amused with fun quilting designs is easily done!

PAINTFALLS
by Angela Walters

I don't often piece quilts. I'd much rather machine quilt, but every once in awhile I get a wild notion to make a quilt. *Paintfalls* was an interesting experience for me. It was my first time using shot cottons and freezer-paper templates. I drew the whole quilt on big pieces of freezer paper before I pieced it! I'm not sure I will ever do that again, but I'm sure glad I tried it once.

This was my first attempt at a "modern" quilt. Up to this point I had never used solid fabrics, so it was a challenge for me. Thankfully, my friend Jacquie Gering helped me pick out some great colors. When it came to the quilting, I had a fun time with the different textures in each of the colors.

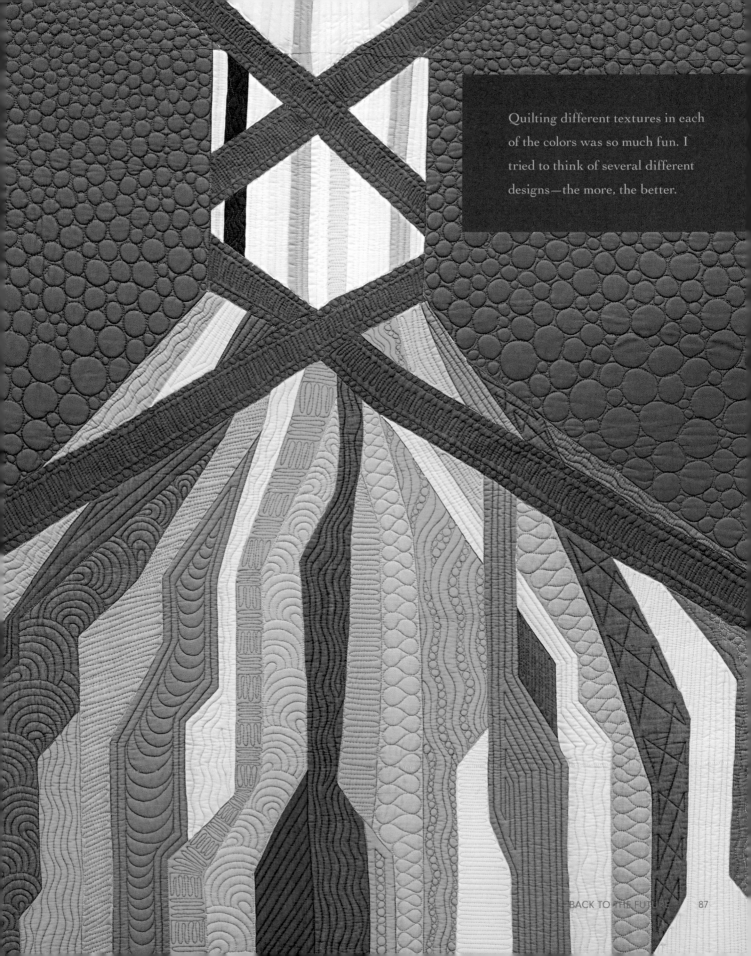

TESSELLATION

designed by Nydia Kehnle

Using quilting to blend blocks together has always been one
of my go-to quilting techniques!

LAUREL
by Angela Walters

When it comes to making my own quilt tops, I love to use fusibile interfacing to adhere pieces onto the top, using the quilting to secure them. Quick piecing means more time for the quilting—my favorite part! For this quilt, I cut out leaf-shaped pieces and arranged them to resemble a laurel. Once I was happy with the layout, I quilted swirls and motifs to fill in the rest.

While I normally use a thread color that blends in with the quilt top, sometimes I like to change it up a bit. Using a thicker gold thread to quilt around the leaves helps them stand out from the background quilting.

LAUREL by Angela Walters

When I'm quilting motifs, such as this swirl, I don't focus on perfection. Instead of trying to make it perfect, I aim for symmetry. Symmetry makes it look perfect even if it isn't!

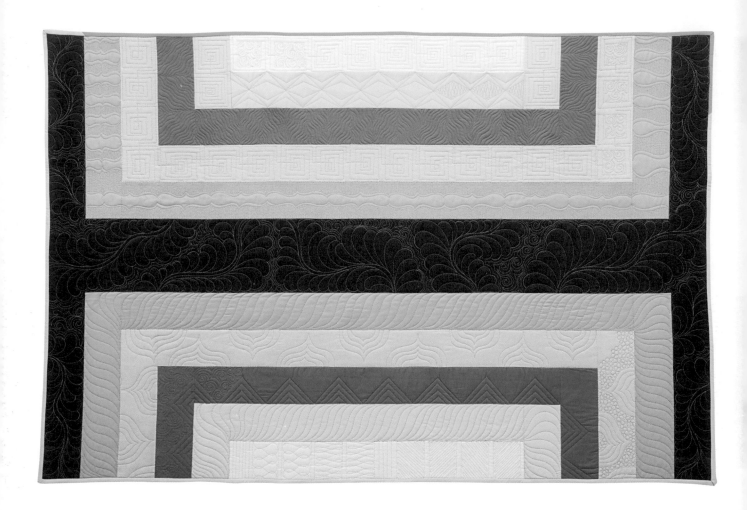

BORDERED
by Angela Walters

The borders of a quilt are my least favorite part of the quilt to work on. That's why it's kind of ironic that this quilt is one of my favorites. It's a great example of how you can use several different designs on a quilt without overwhelming the quilt top.

FLOWER POPS
designed by Alex Anderson

Bright fabrics on a white background is the perfect recipe for a happy quilt. Working with quilts that have a lot of elements, such as appliqué and piecing, is a great opportunity to try out some different quilting techniques. In this quilt, I combined echo quilting with geometric lines and feathers. The contrast between these types of designs is what makes them stand out from each other.

FLOWER POPS
designed by Alex Anderson

Quilting diagonal lines that
go from point to point of the
chevrons is a fun alternative
to regular echo quilting.

NIGHT SKY

designed by Julie Herman, pieced by Ruth Doss

When picking out quilting designs, I like to consider the secondary designs they can make when placed next to each other. Star blocks are a great way to see those secondary designs come to life. Quilting blocks is just half the fun; I also enjoy using different quilting fillers for the backgrounds.

WAVELENGTH
designed by Rebecca Bryan

Deciding on what area of the quilt to highlight can be difficult.
But that definitely wasn't the case for *Wavelength*. I knew instantly
that I wanted to show off the bright and bold shapes of the blocks
in the center.

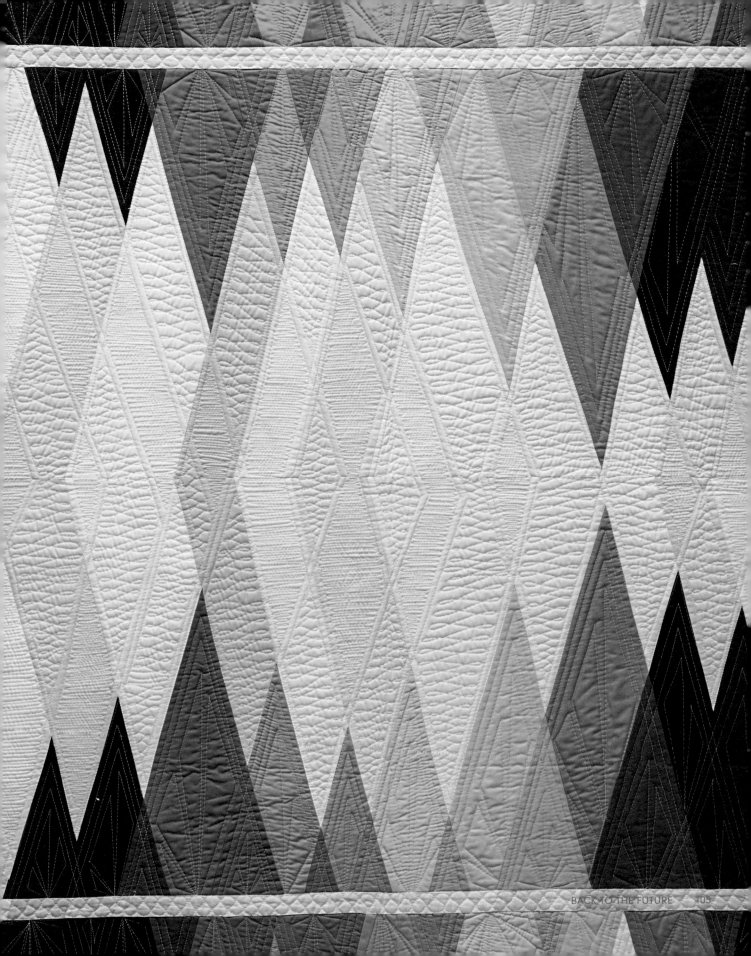

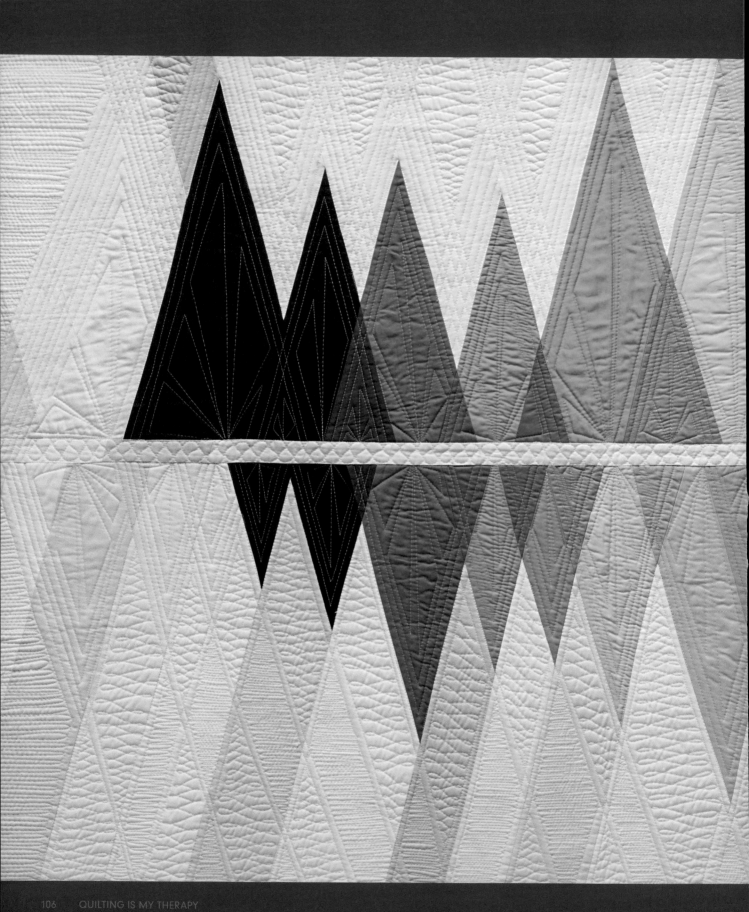

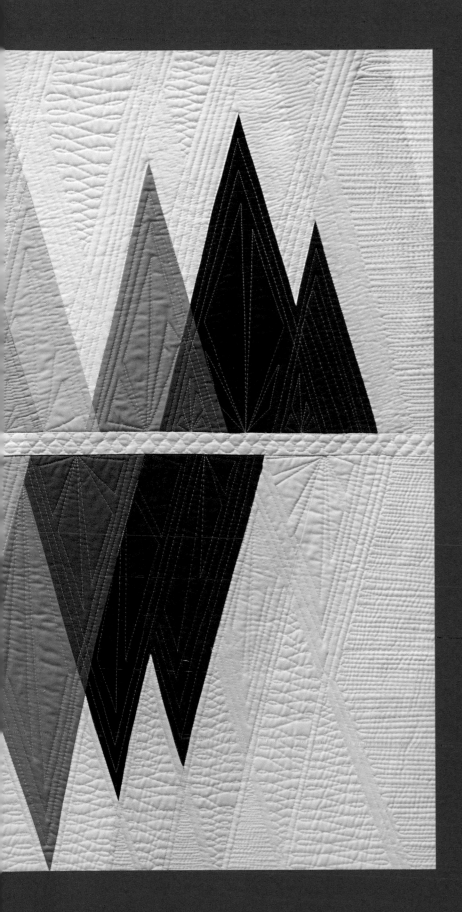

WAVELENGTH
designed by Rebecca Bryan

TEXTURED STRIPES
by Angela Walters

When all you want to do is machine quilt, piecing a basic stripe quilt top is the way to go. Made for a machine quilting class on negative space, this quilt shows a bunch of different designs and techniques. Even though there is a lot of quilting on the quilt, it still has gorgeous quilted texture.

When deciding on which filler quilting designs to use around a swirl chain, I first ask myself how happy I am with the way that it turned out. If I love how it looks, I use a dense filler (such as back-and-forth matchstick quilting) to really make the swirls stand out!

ABOUT THE AUTHOR

Angela Walters is a machine quilter and author who loves to teach others to use quilting to bring out the best in their quilts. Her work has been published in numerous magazines and books. She shares tips and finished quilts on her blog, quiltingismytherapy.com, and believes that "quilting is the funnest part!"

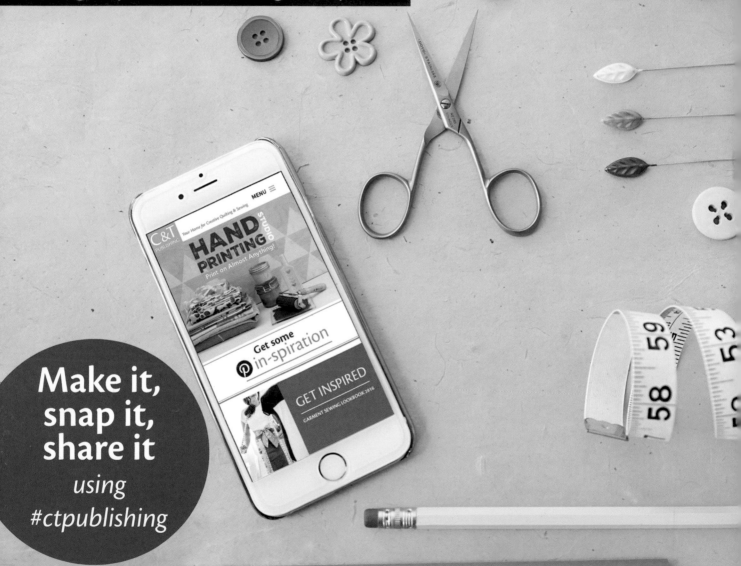